The Farmington Community Library

Donated by

**The Farmington Friends
of the Library**

A *fashionable* HISTORY of COATS & PANTS

A FASHIONABLE HISTORY OF COATS &
PANTS
was produced by

David West 🏃🏃 Children's Books
7 Princeton Court
55 Felsham Road
London SW15 1AZ

This edition first published in the United States in
2003 by Raintree, a division of Reed Elsevier, Inc.,
Chicago, Illinois.

For information address the publisher:
Raintree
100 N. LaSalle
Suite 1200
Chicago, IL 60602

Author: Helen Reynolds
Editors: Clare Hibbert, Marta Segal Block
Picture Research: Carlotta Cooper
Designer: Julie Joubinaux

Library of Congress Cataloging-in-Publication Data:
Reynolds, Helen.
  Coats and pants / Helen Reynolds.
    p. cm. -- (A Fashionable history of costume)
Summary: Looks at the history of coats and pants.
  ISBN 1-4109-0032-0 (Library Binding-Hardcover)
  1. Coats--Juvenile literature. 2. Pants--Juvenile literature. [1.
Coats. 2. Pants.] I. Title. II. Series.
  GT2079.R49 2003
  391.4--dc21
                        2002153948

ISBN 1-4109-0032-0

07 06 05 04 03
10 9 8 7 6 5 4 3 2 1

Printed and bound in China

PHOTO CREDITS:

Abbreviations: t-top, m-middle, b-bottom, r-right,
l-left, c-center.

The publisher would like to thank the following for
permission to reproduce photographs:
Front cover m & 16-17t, tl & 16bm, r & 10r –
Mary Evans Picture Library; pages 3 & 8-9, 4tr &
6tl, 6bl & r, 8tl, 10l & tm, 11tl & tr, 12l, tm & r,
16l, 18bl, 18-19, 19tr & l, 20tl &bl, 26tl & r –
Mary Evans Picture Library; pages 16-17t – Mary
Evans/Lesley Bradshaw Collection; pages 4br, 7tr &
bl, 8bl, 11bl, 14m, 22l, 22tr – Dover Books; pages
4-5b, 15br, 27br, 28br, 29tr – Corbis Images; pages
5tr, 24tr – The Culture Archive; 5br, 11br, 13ml &
tr, 15tr & bl, 17bl, 19br, 21 all, 22br, 23 all, 25tr
& bl, 27l – Rex Features Ltd; page 7br – Digital
Stock; page 7tl – The Kobal Collection/20th
Century Fox; page 9tr – The Kobal Collection/Scott
Free/Enigma/Paramount; page 17tr – The Kobal
Collection/Warner Bros; page 26bl – The Kobal
Collection/Associated British; page 12bm – Karen
Augusta, www.antique-fashion.com; page 14l - ©
National Trust Photographic Library/John
Hammond; page 18br - © National Trust
Photographic Library/Andreas von Einsiedel; pages
20-21m - © National Trust Photographic Library.

A *fashionable* HISTORY of COATS & PANTS

Contents

Saxon mantle

This Saxon king is wearing a mantle—a loose-fitting cloak that wrapped around the shoulders for warmth.

Tartan suit

The traditional suit is a pair of pants with matching jacket. This one is made from tartan, a popular, checked fabric made from woven wool.

From Capes to Combats

In their simplest form, pants and coats can be traced back to the loincloth and to the T-shaped tunic worn as outerwear. Refined by different cultures over time, these basic garments are still recognizable in many areas of the world, including India and the Middle East. In the West, clothing similar to modern pants and coats first appeared in the 17th century. In the 18th and 19th centuries, advances in tailoring techniques further refined these garments. Today with so many fabrics and styles, coats and pants can be very simple —or extremely complex.

JEANS

Once worn only as work wear, over the last five decades jeans have become the most popular pants for any time of day.

MODERN MATERIALS

This ski suit is made with Gore-Tex™, a human-made fabric designed for sports clothes that is waterproof, but also allows the skin to breathe. For high visibility, this suit also has reflective yellow panels.

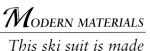

CAMOUFLAGE COMBATS

Originally designed for soldiers in the army, multi-pocketed, baggy combats are now fashionable for both sexes.

From Cloak to Cape

The first cloaks were simple pieces of cloth that wrapped around the body. Cloaks, in one form or another, were worn by the earliest civilizations. Loose cloaks remained the main outer garment until the Middle Ages. After that, the cloak was shaped to fit more snugly over the shoulders, arms, and body.

Ornate copes & capes

Medieval men and women wore a cope—a form of cape with a hook in front and a hood. This garment was also adopted by the clergy. The clergy's copes were sleeveless and lavishly embroidered. Even today, many cathedrals still have a cope chest where they store these clothes.

Short, embroidered capes were fashionable for men of the Renaissance. But from the 1700s, men began to wear coats rather than capes.

Overcoat

Some coats had built-in capes for extra protection against the rain. This one is from 1810.

Kingly cloak

Saxon clothes were simple but colorful. This mid-9th century monarch's scarlet mantle is pinned at the left shoulder.

COSTUME de COUR 1588

Short & showy

Renaissance cloaks were worn indoors as well as out. They were decorative, rather than warm.

SHERLOCK HOLMES

The caped overcoat is often known as a "Sherlock Holmes coat." The fictional detective wore a tweed one, with a matching deerstalker hat.

Women's capes & cloaks

Women wore cloaks until the 20th century. They switched to coats as their clothes became more fitted. Then, in the 1950s, there was a brief fashion for capes as evening wear. French couturier Pierre Balmain (1914–1982) designed Russian-style capes while, in the United States, Pauline Trigère (1912–2002) introduced soft, woolen capes.

Traditional capes, such as ponchos, became fashionable with young people in the late 1960s. This look was revived in the early 21st century.

OVERSIZED OUTERWEAR

In the 1800s women wore hooded cloaks or lacy shawls. Later, when enormous skirts became popular, outer garments had to be amply sized.

OPERA CLOAK

Men's capes were popular evening wear in the 1800s. Opera cloaks were worn over full evening dress.

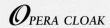

TRADITIONAL SOUTH AMERICAN PONCHOS

The poncho, from South America, is a form of cape. It is a simple rectangle of fabric, with a hole cut for the head.

Doublets to Bomber Jackets

Doublets were first worn by men in the 1300s. They were close-fitting, waisted jackets with detachable sleeves. From the 1400s doublets were padded with wool or horsehair. Padding kept the wearer warm—and also gave him a macho physique. Doublets were often slashed, so that the shirt underneath poked through. They remained popular until the 1600s.

Peasecods

Around 1575 peasecod-bellied doublets came into fashion. They had extra padding at the front— so the wearer seemed to have a pot-belly.

Knightly Attire

These knights of the 1440s wore doublets. The padding offered some protection against enemy arrows.

Vests

From the 1500s gentlemen wore sleeveless jackets, called jerkins. By the 1700s a sleeveless undercoat, later to be called a vest, was also popular. It reached the knee, but soon shortened. Men left their coats unbuttoned to show off their dazzling vests. Even in the 1800s, when men's clothes became rather somber, vests remained fancy— although they now matched the pants or jacket.

Women's Vests

Vests were part of traditional women's dress, especially in areas of Eastern Europe. In the late 1800s, working women began to wear masculine vests with the new jacket-and-skirt suits.

The short jackets worn by 19th-century hussars were tight fitting. In the 20th century, military jackets were cut more generously. They also came in colors such as khaki, that gave far better camouflage.

Styles for soldiers & civilians

Now widely worn as casual wear, bomber jackets were first designed for fighter pilots in World War II.

Until about 1900 military jackets were modeled on the doublet, but their close fit hampered movement. By World War I (1914–1918), roomier, hip-length battle jackets were worn instead. New jackets developed for soldiers in World War II (1939–1945) included the Eisenhower and bomber jackets, both of which came in wool or leather. The Eisenhower jacket was named after Dwight Eisenhower (1890–1969), Supreme Commander of Allied Forces and later our 34th President. It had stylish epaulettes (shoulder straps), and stopped at the waist with a buttoned belt. The bomber jacket was worn by pilots. It had an elastic waist and zipped up at the front. Both these styles were adapted for civilian wear after the war, and are still popular today.

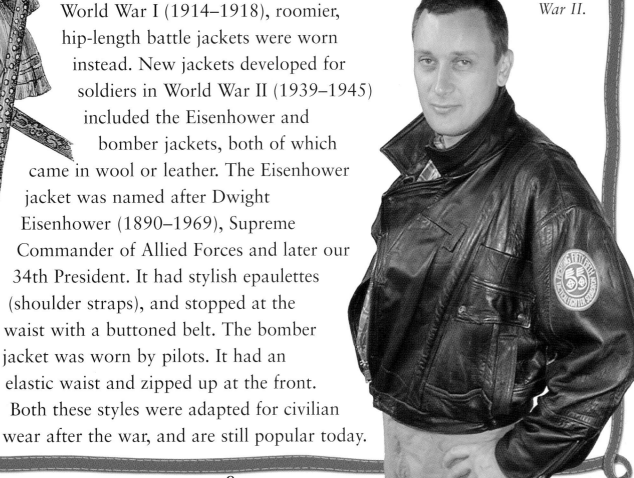

Breeches & Plus-Fours

Breeches developed from the trunk-hose worn in the 16th century. These consisted of puffed-out trunks that came to mid-thigh, and stockings (hose) that covered the rest of the leg. By the 17th century, trunks had lengthened to become breeches. Men wore breeches until around 1850, though at the end they were only worn at royal courts.

Nobleman

This 1789 British gentleman wears striped silk stockings and slim, gold breeches. Under the frock-coat, suspenders hold up the breeches.

Venetians

Both trunk-hose and breeches were worn in the late 16th century. These men wear Venetians, a style of breeches.

The 1600s

Full, knickerbocker-style breeches had strings that tied at the back of the waist. Then, in the late 1600s, suspenders were introduced. The new invention meant that breeches could be narrower and have a looser waistband.

Petticoat breeches

These petticoat breeches of 1630 originated in France. The full leg looked like a skirt or petticoat—especially if trimmed with frilly lace!

$\mathscr{P}$LUS-FOURS

In the 1920s, tweed plus-fours were often teamed with a patterned Fair Isle sweater and matching socks.

$\mathscr{B}$reeches come back!

By the 1920s, men wanted more comfortable styles, especially for sports. They adopted plus-fours, which were like breeches, only longer and fuller. Their name referred to the extra four inches (10 centimeters) of cloth beneath the knee. The Prince of Wales (1894–1972) made plus-fours popular after wearing them to play golf. The knickerbocker look was revived in the 1970s, only this time for women rather than men.

$\mathscr{C}$ASUAL CLOTHES IN THE UNITED STATES

This young American of 1927 has the relaxed and easy look of knickerbockers, sports jacket and tie, and a button-up vest.

$\mathscr{B}$REECHES FOR SPORTS

Breeches were part of the usual uniform for 19th-century sports.

$\mathscr{S}$PANISH BULLFIGHTER IN BREECHES

Today bullfighters still wear colorful brocade breeches in the bullring. A matching jacket and scarlet cape complete the look.

Pants

In the 1800s, long pants began to replace breeches for everyday wear. They were held up with suspenders and had stirrup-style straps that went under the shoe. Fly fronts, with buttons, not zippers, first appeared in 1823. They became widespread in the 1840s, about the same time that pants became straighter.

Neat creases

Pants were always pressed with the crease at the side, along the seam. Front-creased pants only came into fashion in the early 1900s, after the invention of the pants press.

Dandy

These pants of 1826 were cut generously over the hip and thigh, then skin-tight below the knee.

Fancy suspenders

Suspenders are straps that hold up the pants. These floral ones are from the 1800s.

Saxon trousers

This Saxon warrior wore wool stockings and leg bandages. He would have worn braies beneath his tunic.

Russian style

Pants based on those worn by the Russian cavalry were fashionable in the early 1800s. Cossack pants had a pleated waist and narrow legs.

Pants for young followers of fashion

The 1950s saw the birth of many youth fashions. With more spending money than ever before, young people no longer dressed just like their parents. The British mod look of the early 1960s was all about being snappily dressed—and that meant dark suits with short jackets and tight drainpipe pants.

In the late 1960s, a completely new pants style emerged that appealed to both men and women. Cut low and tight around the hips, these bell bottom pants flared out from the thighs. Flares came back into fashion in the late 1990s.

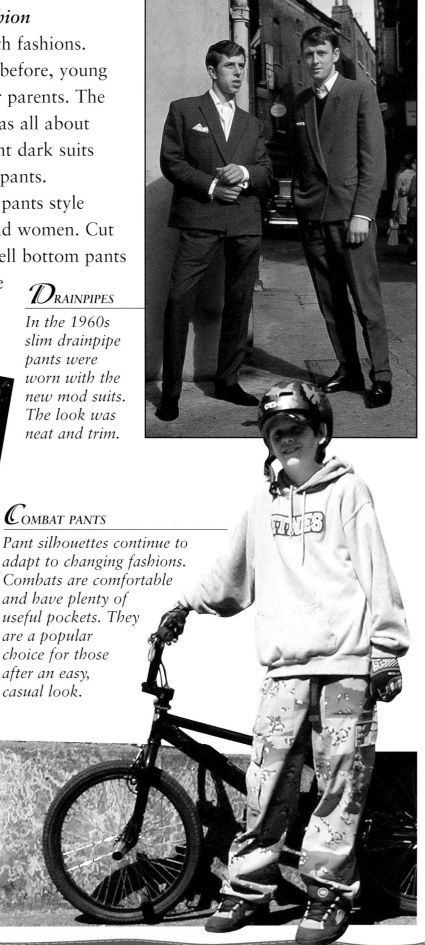

Drainpipes

In the 1960s slim drainpipe pants were worn with the new mod suits. The look was neat and trim.

Combat pants

Pant silhouettes continue to adapt to changing fashions. Combats are comfortable and have plenty of useful pockets. They are a popular choice for those after an easy, casual look.

Flares hit the dance floor

Flares were fashionable in the 1970s. John Travolta (1954–) famously danced in a flared suit in the film Saturday Night Fever *(1974).*

Baggy Pants

Popular in the Middle East for centuries, baggy pants were not widely worn in the West until the 20th century. Except for braies, which were an early form of long johns, modern long pants did not appear until the 1800s.

Where to stop?

Most long pants stop at the ankle. Not so with those in this Samurai-style costume—or with 21st-century teenagers!

Wide boys

The 19th-century fashion for slim-fitting pants lasted until the early 1920s. Then, pants were cut with a wider leg and cuffs were added to the hem. This fashion was taken to extremes by some students at Oxford University. They wore baggy trousers that measured 20 in (50 cm) across at the bottom hem. Before long, wide pants like these were nicknamed Oxford bags. The style was adopted by young women in the 1930s and 1970s.

Styles for a traveler

Thomas Legh (1792–1857) explored the Nile in 1812. He wore baggy North African pants for this portrait, rather than the slim fashions of the day.

Fashions from Hollywood

Wide pants for men remained popular thoughout the 1930s, thanks to the relaxed tailoring worn by Hollywood stars such as Clark Gable (1901–1960) and Humphrey Bogart (1899–1957). Around this time, belts replaced suspenders. Belted pants sat lower on the hip, so they looked even baggier.

In the 1940s and 1950s, there was a craze among Latinos and African Americans for zoot suits. These had extremely baggy trousers that tapered in at the bottom. The style never really caught on in Europe, where fabrics were still in short supply after the war.

Zoot suit

The zoot suit used lots of fabric for its full, baggy pants and wide-shouldered jacket. The style was popular with jazz musicians, such as Cab Calloway (1907–1994), shown right.

Gangster chic

In the 1930s, Chicago gangsters were known for their trademark baggy suits and trilby hats. This modern version doesn't always come with a fake machine gun!

Baggy boarder

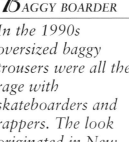

In the 1990s oversized baggy trousers were all the rage with skateboarders and rappers. The look originated in New York, but soon spread across the world.

In her newspaper, The Lily,
Amelia Bloomer called on
all sensible women to
adopt this outfit.

Women in Pants

In the early 1850s, Elizabeth Smith Miller (1822–1911) noticed that women in Swiss health spas wore Turkish trousers under short, loose dresses. She decided to adopt the same outfit, encouraging her cousin, Elizabeth Cady Stanton (1815–1902), and Amelia Bloomer (1818–1894) to do the same. The bloomer outfit was born.

The short-lived fashion for bloomers

Worn without a corset, the bloomer outfit was comfortable as well as practical. It was very popular with early feminists. Unfortunately they were widely ridiculed. By 1860 the outfit was dropped so that women's rights activists would be taken seriously.

PANTSUIT OF 1919

After World War I, it became more acceptable for women to wear pants.

DRESSED FOR CYCLING

The bicycle, photographed here in 1896, was a new and popular invention. Cylcling was difficult in a full skirt, so divided skirts were designed.

Slacks for beatniks

Actress Audrey Hepburn (1928–1993) starred as a beatnik (bohemian) in Funny Face (1957). By the 1950s, well-cut pants were part of every fashionable young woman's wardrobe. It took another decade for pants to be worn by older women.

Forties Pantsuits

In the early 1940s, many women signed up for war work away from home. Freer than ever before, some adopted masculine pants, shirts, and jackets for everyday wear.

Overalls

Overalls were originally worn by working men. In World War II, they were worn by women working in factories.

Pushing for change

During the 1880s the newly formed Rational Dress Society promoted a bifurcated garment, that is, a divided skirt or culottes. This became popular with lady cyclists, but was not accepted by the general public. In one famous court case, a judge ruled that it was all right for a hotel to deny service to a woman in a bifurcated garment.

World War I changed all this. Taking over men's jobs, women also began to wear masculine pants for both work and play. In World War II, factory workers routinely wore them. Today pants are a key part of women's casual and formal dress.

Dress Coats

Dress, or frock, coats are tight-fitting, formal coats that have tails at the back and a cutaway or square front. First worn in the late 18th century, they evolved into modern morning coats (worn in the day) and dinner jackets (for evening).

Frocks to show off in

In the late 18th century, the full-skirted frock coats worn for riding were adapted in finer fabrics. Popular in the royal courts of Europe, these lavishly embroidered frock coats were unbuttoned to display colorful vests. About 1800 fashionable frock coats were double breasted and worn with a large cravat. By 1850 frock coats were plain and dark, but with shiny, satin lapels.

Day coat

With a cutaway front and broad, square tails, this frock coat of 1829 is typical of the time. It is worn with instep pants, square-toed shoes, and a top hat.

Velvet frock-coat

This maroon frock coat of 1770 had a matching vest and breeches. Silk stockings covered the legs.

Napoleonic style

After the Revolution (1789) frock coats in France were less showy—but the clothes underneath were not!

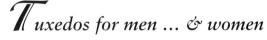
Tuxedos for men ... & women

In the 1880s a tailless black dinner jacket became popular for less formal occasions. In the United States, it was named the tuxedo, after the Tuxedo Club in New Jersey; elsewhere it was called a smoking jacket.

In 1966 Yves Saint Laurent (1936–) introduced tuxedos as evening wear for women. These have come in and out of fashion ever since.

Walking coat

Also of 1829 this variation of the frock coat does not cut away at the front, but is one length all the way around.

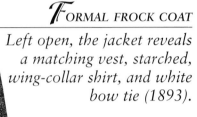

Formal frock coat

Left open, the jacket reveals a matching vest, starched, wing-collar shirt, and white bow tie (1893).

Morning coat

In the early 20th century, morning coats were worn to the office. Today they are reserved for formal occasions.

Dinner jackets today

With their white front, it's easy to see why tuxedos are nicknamed "penguin suits."

Suits You, Sir

At the end of the 18th century, men in the United States started to wear a version of the frock coat that had a short, or bob, tail. Known as the bob coat, it was the first garment to resemble the modern suit jacket.

Lounging about

By 1860 some men were wearing a three-piece suit made up of a lounging jacket, matching vest, and pants. The loose cut of the jacket was very different from the snug-fitting frock-coat or morning coat. Their informality made lounge suits very popular with artists, bohemians, and intellectuals.

By the beginning of the 20th century, the lounge suit had become the accepted informal suit, especially among the young and fashionable. Accessories became more relaxed too, with felt Homburg hats replacing the traditional black silk topper.

Frock-coat

These stuffy and restrictive formal frock-coats (1839) would soon give way to lounge suits.

Comic dandies

Like many new fashions, lounge suits were considered too outlandish at first. In this cartoon of 1869, the two men wearing modern, loose-cut suits are made to appear ridiculous.

Relaxed royalty

The Prince of Wales, later Edward VIII, on vacation with friends. In their light lounge suits and Homburg hats, they look far more relaxed than the gentleman in the stiff, formal frock-coat.

Lounge suits for one & all

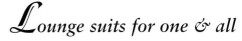

By the 1920s it was acceptable for professional men to wear lounge suits to work, while others wore them to church on Sundays. Lounge suits are still worn, but details such as the width of the lapels, pant style, or even the thickness of the shoulder pads, continue to change.

*D*OUBLE-BREASTED SUIT

This scene is from the gangster movie, Public Enemy (1931). Double-breasted jackets became popular during the 1920s.

*D*RESSED FOR THE CITY

By 1960 suits and ties were standard for the office. Accessories included a trilby or bowler hat and an umbrella.

*S*AFARI SUIT

Lightweight safari suits have long been worn in hot climates. Here Roger Moore, as James Bond, wears a flared-leg version (1978).

LUXURY COAT, 1800s

Fur was a favorite choice for coats and trimmings. Today wearing real fur is generally seen as socially unacceptable.

Overcoats & Anoraks

Coats not only provide extra warmth, they also give protection from the rain. In 1823, the chemist Charles Macintosh (1766–1843) patented a fabric of wool and india-rubber—the first human-made waterproof fabric.

Early raincoats

Macintosh's company sold the first rubber macintoshes, or raincoats. Until the 1850s, this was the only waterproof human-made material for coats.

ARCTIC ANORAKS

The earliest-known weatherproof coats were hooded, seal-gut anoraks. Worn by the Inuit, they repelled water and snow.

The overcoat

The overcoat first appeared in the 1700s. This loose, long-sleeved coat had overlapping shoulder capes to help keep the clothes underneath dry. The style was popular with dandies and drivers alike. Horseriders had a special version with a back slit. Both styles are still worn today.

COATS IN THE TRENCHES

Not everyone fighting in World War I wore a trench coat. This French soldier wears an overcoat, which was much plainer in style.

PARKAS

Parkas were popular in the 1960s, and came back into fashion in the 1990s. Longer than jackets, they have large hoods, sometimes fur-trimmed.

CROMBIE COATS

During the Civil War, the British company Crombie made coats for the Confederate Army. They are still making similar coats today. Crombie is a soft, thick, wool fabric.

Trench coats

In the 19th century, a military style overcoat with epaulettes first made its appearance. In World War I, a weatherproof version of this was issued to British soldiers. After the war it was adapted for everyday wear. Trench coats worn today have barely changed. Made in wool or gabardine, they have epaulettes and wide lapels, and are belted at the waist.

ANORAKS

A pullover hooded jacket long enough to cover the hips is known as an anorak.

TRENCH RAINCOATS

In the Pink Panther films, Peter Sellers (1925–1980) was Inspector Clouseau, a bumbling detective. He always wore a classic, trench-style raincoat.

23

Jeans & Denim

In the 1850s Levi Strauss (1829–1902) began selling riveted denim jeans, which he called "waist overalls," to California gold prospectors. Denim is a thick cotton fabric that was originally woven in Nîmes, France—its name comes from the French, de Nîmes (from Nîmes). In the 1850s denim was practically unknown; today, it is highly fashionable, and seemingly indispensable.

Anti-fashion for rebels

Westerns of the 1930s had starred cowboys in jeans, but the garment really took off about 1950. Rebellious teenagers adopted workwear because it was cheap and tough. Besides Levi's, Wrangler and Lee jeans were also big sellers. Jeans were worn by bikers, musicians, and film stars, notably Elvis Presley (1935–1977), and James Dean (1931–1955).

The mark of the individual

By the late 1960s, everyone was wearing jeans. Young people began to customize theirs, sewing on paisley patches, or painting on flowers, while civil rights activists added buttons that advertised their cause. A decade later, punk rockers wore distressed jeans with rips and zippers in odd places.

Denim haute couture

Denim had been used in the late 1930s by the American designer Claire McCardell (1905–1958) for sporty playsuits. In the late 1970s, Perry Ellis (1940–1986), Calvin Klein (1942–), and Gloria Vanderbilt (1924–) began to design jeans that were chic—and expensive. Pierre Cardin (1922–), Ralph Lauren (1939–), and Giorgio Armani (1934–) soon added jeans to their collections. Today denim is mainstream fashion worn by young, middle-aged, and old alike in both figure-hugging and relaxed styles.

ROCKERS

First worn as workwear, jeans were adopted by young people in the 1950s. Rockers teamed jeans with t-shirts and leather jackets.

21ST-CENTURY JEANS

Madonna displayed the cowboy look, wearing a relaxed, checked shirt and jeans for the video of her song Don't Tell Me *(2000).*

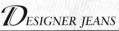

DESIGNER JEANS

These jeans by Armani have a leather patch on the waistband. It is a copy of the one used on original Levi's.

Shorts

In the first half of the 20th century, both men and women started to wear shorts for sports and as casual wear. Starting in the 1920s, they were also the standard pants for young boys, whatever the weather. In Britain they remain a part of some school uniforms.

Short pants

At the beginning of the 20th century, it became fashionable for men to wear shorts when visiting warmer climates. White Bermuda shorts (shorts that reach the knee) are still worn in the tropics by sailors. Lord Baden Powell (1857–1941), founder of the World Scout Movement, made gabardine khaki shorts part of the boy scout uniform.

In the 1930s there were attempts to replace pants with shorts. There was even a brief craze for satin evening shorts, but the idea never really caught on! Today, shorts remain popular warm-weather clothing for both boys and men.

AUSTRIAN PEASANT IN LEDERHOSEN, 1889

Leather shorts, or lederhosen, were popular in countries such as Switzerland, Austria, and Germany for centuries. They were held up by suspenders.

DESERT SHORTS

This scene is from Ice Cold in Alex *(1958) a World War II movie set in North Africa. The heroes wear the usual hot-climate attire— gabardine shorts.*

FIFTIES SHORTS

Shorts became popular with young women in the 1950s. This pair is modeled by French actress Nicole Maurey (1925–).

Shorter & shorter

In the 1950s young women wore short, figure-hugging cotton shorts as casual wear. The look was an instant hit because it showed off the legs.

In the early 1970s, hot pants came in. These were the shortest shorts ever, often worn with long socks or high boots to draw even more attention to the legs.

In the 1970s and 1980s, tailored shorts were sometimes combined with jackets for work, but shorts remain an item of casual clothing.

Multi-purpose

These pants are ideal for unpredictable climates. If the sun comes out, the legs zip off for instant shorts!

Hot pants

These super-short shorts were very fashionable in the early 1970s. Denim hot pants were home-made, by cutting off old jeans. They were known as Daisy Dukes, after a TV show character.

Lycra

In the late 1980s, Lycra was added to cycling shorts. The tight fit reduces air resistance, allowing higher speeds.

Fashionable Technology

Until the mid-19th century, pants were pull-ons, held up with suspenders. Then, tailors developed the fly front, which concealed a row of buttons. Pants could fit more tightly at the waist and belts began to replace suspenders. Button-flies remained popular until the 1930s, when zippers came in.

Today's pants

The zipper is still the preferred fastening for pants. However, some jeans use the old button-fly and appeal to customers in search of a retro look. Suspenders, too, still have their place in fashion. The pants of modern dress-suits have waistband buttons for attaching suspenders, which these days are made using up-to-date stretchy Lycra.

The zipper

The original zipper, patented in 1893, was large and bulky. It took several decades to produce a zipper that was light enough to be used in clothes.

Absolutely riveting!

Copper rivets were first put on jeans in 1873. They stop the seams of bulging pockets from stretching.

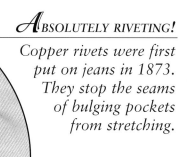

Non-rip material

Torn pants are a thing of the past with the latest, tough sports fabrics. The material in these nonrip shorts has strong, cross-hatched threads woven into it so a rip cannot spread.

Fabrics for the great outdoors

The quest for weatherproof coats and jackets began when Macintosh patented his rubber mix for raincoats in the 1800s. The first waterproofs kept off the rain but were also heavy, smelled bad when wet, and did not allow body moisture to escape.

Today's designers use a range of light, weatherproof fabrics. Polartec fleece was introduced in 1981, and is still being improved—Polartec Power Shield (2002) is wind-and water-resistant. Gore-Tex™, which was patented in the 1970s, remains one of the best waterproof fabrics, popular for ski suits and other sportswear. In labs around the world scientists are creating the next generation of high-tech fabrics.

How Gore-Tex™ works

The special feature of Gore-Tex™ is a waterproof skin covered in billions of tiny holes, or pores. No rain can penetrate, because each pore is 20,000 times smaller than a raindrop. However, the pores are also 700 times bigger than a molecule of sweat. This means that moisture can evaporate outward through the fabric. The wearer can be as active as he or she likes, whatever the weather, without getting damp from rain—or sweat!

Windproof

Waterproof

Body moisture escapes

Outer shell

Micro-porous, breathable "skin"

Inner lining

Timeline

Prehistory
The first garment for the lower half of the body was the loincloth.

The ancient world
The ancient Egyptians took the loincloth and passed it through the legs to produce an early pant-like garment.

The Middle Ages
The Celts and Saxons had worn pant-like garments called braies, but by 1200 C.E. they were concealed under the long tunic. A cloak called a mantle gave extra protection against the elements. In the 1400s men wore both long and short tunics and stockings (hose) covered the legs. The mantle developed into a fitted, semicircular cloak called a cope, which draped over the shoulders. The clergy wore decorative copes.

16th century
In the early 1500s, men wore padded doublets over their shirts. These were sometimes slashed to display the white undershirt. The upper half of the hose developed into the "trunk," which looked like puffed-out shorts and which, like the doublet, was padded. Over the doublet a loose, unfitted jerkin was worn. Jerkins fell to just above the knee. Some had full sleeves, others were sleeveless. Toward the end of the century, the jerkin was replaced by a short, full cloak.

17th century
Men's trunks grew longer and became knee breeches. A full version, known as petticoat breeches, became popular and was often trimmed with lace. Doublets became longer and looser.

18th century
Breeches became narrow, and were now worn with vests and knee-length jackets that had wide sleeves. The overcoat was the most fashionable outerwear for men. At the end of the century, men's clothes became less showy, although fine silks and brocades were still worn at royal court. The square-fronted frock coat with tails and short-tailed bob coat were introduced.

19th century
Pants replaced knee breeches. The morning coat became the most popular formal day jacket, while the frock coat was incorporated into evening wear. In the 1850s a number of radical ladies started wearing the bloomer suit—a relatively short dress worn with Turkish trousers. The lounge suit was worn by men from the 1860s as informal day wear; for evening wear, the dinner jacket or tuxedo was introduced in the 1880s. In the 1870s Levi Strauss took out a patent on his denim pants, later to be known as jeans.

20th century & beyond
By the 1920s, women were wearing pants, especially for sports. Clothing for both sexes became more casual and men adopted sports jackets. Men's pants had cuffs and were wider—the widest were known as Oxford bags. In the 1950s, suits with tight drainpipe pants became fashionable. Jeans were worn by both sexes. In the 1970s flares, or bell-bottoms became popular. At the end of the decade, the punk movement gave birth to an aggressive, scruffy look. Since the 1980s many styles of coats and pants have coexisted. Suit jackets in the 1980s had big, padded shoulders to project a powerful image. Youth styles have ranged from oversized skate pants to the distressed, anti-fashion look known as grunge. Sports clothes are now popular with many people. Jackets and leggings in human-made materials such as fleecy Polartec, weatherproof Gore-Tex™, and stretchy Lycra are an important part of many everyday wardrobes. Padded vests are often worn for extra warmth. And more than a century later, denim jeans remain the most popular pants of all.

$\mathcal{G}$lossary

braies garment worn under a man's tunic to cover the legs

bell-bottoms pants that flare widely at the ankle

brocade fabric, often silk, with a raised, usually floral-motif pattern

couturier person who designs fashionable, custom-made clothing

crinoline wide skirts worn starting in 1850s, which were supported on a frame of stiff hoops

cuffs bottom hem on a pair of pants

double-breasted coat or jacket that has a double line of buttons at the front opening

gabardine dense fabric that has a fine diagonal rib effect, popular for suits, coats, pants, and shorts

Gore-Tex™ human-made, breathable fabric used for weatherproof jackets, pants, and other articles of clothing

haute couture French for "high dressmaking." These garments are constructed to the client's personal measurements. The workmanship of haute couture is usually superb.

instep trousers pants with straps that go over the shoe, also known as stirrup pants

jerkin short, tight-fitting coat of the 16th and 17th centuries

lapels front part of the jacket that turns back on itself, above the buttons

Lycra very stretchy human-made fabric

morning coat plain, dark coats for formal occasions. They have long tails, and the front of the coat slopes toward the tails below waist level.

single-breasted coat or jacket that has a single line of buttons at the front opening

tails back part of a coat that extends beyond the waist, often as far as the back of the knee

trilby hat soft, felt hat with a dented crown

tweed coarse wool cloth woven into a pattern, popular for coats and suits

Index